A Note from Matt

You are a thought leader. You have **unique perspectives**, **unique experiences**, and **unique talents** that have developed throughout your career that <u>you need to share with the world</u>.

You owe it to yourself, to those closest to you, and to the world to do everything in your power to maximize your potential.

Too many entrepreneurs are 'hoping' that opportunities develop… Not you.

To grow your business and help people in a positive way, you need to have a clearly defined and organized plan to follow.

I love working with people just like you to develop an action plan that will get you moving towards living your life's mission.

As I continue to learn and grow every day, I also know that:

"If it's perfect, it's too late."

The following quote from Brendon Burchard inspired me to stop waiting and start writing:

"If you have something that can change peoples' lives, it's your responsibility to find them. It's not their responsibility to find you."

I've seen how much The MoMachine has helped others… and I know how much it can help you.

What's Inside?

The Journey From 17 To 27 5
What Matt Morse Does.. 17
The 3 Phases of Building Your Online Business 27
What's In This For Me? 35
2 Critical Things to Focus On 43
The 3 Myths of Online Marketing 45
Disclaimer 47
The MoMachine 49
#1) Website 51
#2) Email 57
#3) Social 67
#4) Content 79
#5) Products 83
#6) Launch 87
#7) Funnel 99
#8) Advertising 105
Recap 111
MoTools 115
Matt Morse 121
Kaifect 125
Gratitude 129

Featured Q&A 135
Bonus #1: How To Write a Book in 1 Day 147
Bonus #2: 2 Steps to Get More Speaking Engagements.... 149
Bonus #3: How To Determine Free vs. Paid....................... 151
Bonus #4: What To Do If You Get Frustrated..................... 153
Bonus #5: 5 Bullets for Your Brand or Business.................. 157
Bonus #6: The 2 Most Powerful Tools for MoProductivity .. 163
Bonus #7: How This Book Was Written 167

Copyright © 2018 Matt Morse Companies, LLC.
All rights reserved.
ISBN: 9781790986224

The Journey From 17 To 27

At 17 years old, all I wanted to do was play college baseball and then become a college baseball coach.

Growing up, I had the opportunity to be around great coaches and mentors. I played on elite travel teams with great teammates. After collecting 28 Division 1 baseball scholarship offers, I chose The University of Alabama at Birmingham (UAB).

When I arrived at UAB, I was surrounded by a great coaching staff who really cared about the players and their development both on and off the field. When I stepped on the field at UAB (after being one of the better players on the teams that I was on growing up), I realized:

Everyone on the team was just as good as I was, if not better.

If I wanted to earn a starting position, I needed to find ways to help the team win.

During my time at UAB, I was exposed to the mental side of baseball and had the opportunity to be around some of the best. I knew it could help and was intrigued. (It couldn't hurt, right?) Our coaches hired various speakers and consultants to come in and speak to the team, and encouraged us to read their books, watch their videos, etc…

Since I knew that I wanted to coach after I was done playing, I wanted to learn more about the mental side of the game to develop my own philosophy of what I would teach players in regards to the mental game when I started coaching.

I set out to do an active research type of project where I interviewed some of the leaders in sport psychology, specifically the mental game of baseball, and asked them a series of questions to identify what the common denominators were among what all of these experts were teaching.

Through that process of interviewing these individuals, not only did I learn a ton about sport psychology and the mental game, but **many of the interviewees were encouraging me to turn the content into a book**, or an audio program, so that coaches, players, and parents around the country could get their hands on this information that I was collecting.

Now what?

I knew that the information these experts had shared was very powerful and could really help players, coaches, and parents…

But, how was I going to get it into their hands?

At that time, I realized I needed to learn the self publishing process to package this information into a book. I had the interviews transcribed into text, sorted them by topic, and developed it into a paperback book, eBook, 10-CD set, and digital download.

If I just put the product on Amazon, I would never know who actually bought it and they were going to take 50% of the profits, making it difficult to measure the effectiveness of marketing campaigns.

And, so it began…

Google + YouTube University

I discovered that I needed to:

- buy a domain,
- get a hosting account,
- install WordPress,
- create the graphics,
- design the pages,
- write the copy,

- hook up a shopping cart,
- configure the credit card processor,
- create the template for the confirmation e-mails,
- and find a way to ship them the physical product...

As an NCAA student-athlete, I was not able to use my name or likeness in any way to promote a product or make money at the time so I was forced to get creative in how I would go about getting this project out to the world.

After all that was completed, I needed to drive traffic to my website, so I created a Twitter Account and a Facebook Page. Then, I used those social media accounts to interact with the interviewees and share quotes and snippets from the book to create some interest.

The next day, **I stumbled upon Jeff Walker's book** *Launch* and the lightbulb went off... (I'll explain this further in Part 6 of The MoMachine.)

I read the entire book overnight and hardly slept before an early morning team workout.

The book took the exact ideas I had in mind and put them into a formula that was easy to understand. I knew it wouldn't be easy but was confident that I could find a way to execute.

As a college student with little to no money to work with, **I positioned the launch as a 'pre-order'** and indicated the books would be delivered within 3-4 weeks. That way, I could get the orders in advance and use that money to fund the purchase of the books and CDs.

I scheduled the pre-order to go from the first pitch until the final out of that night's World Series game between the Giants and the Royals…

When the first pitch was thrown, I flipped the switch and my first attempt at creating a 'sales page' went live.

Within 60 seconds, the first order notification came in and I felt a huge sigh of relief… I knew everything was working (and someone felt like what I had created was worth some of their hard earned money).

At that moment, I realized that this online marketing thing was pretty cool.

Cha-ching!

Cha-ching!

Cha-ching!

The orders continued pouring in. (Thanks to the awesome interviewees who had chosen to promote it to their lists!)

Before I knew it, I had a stack of USPS priority mail boxes stacked up in my college apartment. Luckily, my parents were in town from Chicago when they all arrived so they could help me package up the boxes and get them in the mail ASAP. :)

Up until this point, I had been set on becoming a college baseball coach as soon as I was done playing.

That shifted pretty quickly when I saw the opportunity to help people improve their lives through the power of the internet. **I was hooked.**

More than people paying for something I worked hard to create (which was cool), what was even more powerful and inspiring for me was the impact and lives being changed.

One coach even told me that reading this book changed his perspective and saved his marriage.

That's what gets me out of bed in the morning.

I had always wanted to coach college baseball, but I saw a very unique opportunity that **brought together my strengths, my passions, and what unique value** I could bring to the world…

As much as I wanted to teach young athletes how to hit, run, and throw… what intrigued me the most about coaching was the ability to build a 'brand' within a college baseball program, which is why I was always fascinated by the recruiting process.

Through the 'launch' of this first product, I also realized **a large gap in the online marketing world** (of sports, in particular). Soon after, several of the interviewees reached out wanting me to help them promote their products and services in a similar way that I had done with my first product.

While I was still playing for 2 more years at UAB, I continued to dig in, study, and learn more about how I could get better and improve myself so that I can then in turn help others at a high level.

When I was done playing, I had several opportunities to coach at the Division 1 level, which is what I had always wanted to do...

At the same time, I realized that the business opportunities that presented themselves might not always be there if I went into coaching.

I decided to go all in.

Within 2 months after playing my last game at UAB, I finished my MBA, got married, honeymooned in Kauai and somehow talked my wife into giving up her good 'job' with insurance, benefits, and pension to move out to Texas and pursue my entrepreneurial dreams…

Technically, I started 'consulting' with multiple clients, helping them to organize and grow their businesses, create and promote their products and services, find unique and creative ways to stand out from the crowd, etc…

Within the first few days, I knew I made the right choice. I was having a blast.

I really focused on overdelivering for the first clients who trusted me to organize, manage, and grow their business. That led to **positive referrals to other authors, speakers, and coaches** who were in search of the same level of innovation and growth.

At the same time, I was investing countless hours, days, and weeks into studying what was working, and what the leaders in online marketing were teaching.

I attended several events, networked with other individuals in the industry, studied everything I could get my hands on, read every book I could find, and watched hours and hours of online video courses to get a really good understanding of what the online marketing landscape looked like... To this day, I'm always looking for ways to improve so that we can help our clients in bigger, better ways.

I quickly realized that the consulting and the strategy was great, but **what was really lacking was someone in the trenches doing the work**, taking responsibility for creating real results and doing a great job with it, while still being able to maintain the personal connection and understand how each individual business and brand is unique.

Oftentimes, **people are afraid to fail and unsure about what direction to go.** When clients choose to work with us, we collaborate on a game plan that everyone is comfortable with and from there, **we take responsibility for getting it done.** That is one thing that I believe has allowed us to have some great success in a relatively short amount of time.

There's no one cookie cutter approach to what I'm going to share with you... but there are some very important pieces of the puzzle that you need to have in place to maximize your efforts.

So you're probably wondering at this point why you should listen to me....

Since I launched that first product online, I've become obsessed with finding the best possible ways to help people like yourself create similar life-changing experiences.

I've learned the hard way and I hope this book simplifies everything for you so that you can be free to share your message with the world and build the business you've always dreamed of. (It should save you at least 5 years of time and energy that it would take to try and figure all this stuff out on your own.)

What Matt Morse Does

Very often asked, this is a loaded question... but at its very core I wear 4 Hats:

1. Entrepreneur
2. Coach
3. Agent
4. Author/Speaker

While the day to day varies greatly, here's a quick breakdown of what I do:

1) Entrepreneur

I currently own 2 companies, and am a partner in a third. The first is the **Matt Morse Companies**... which is our hands-off coaching and consulting. There are 6 ways that we work with our clients, which I'll explain later on...

Again, what I recognized was missing was: **Who's going to get in the trenches and do the work?** Who's going to construct the website, write the emails, build the audiences, create the social media posts, launch the products, optimize the funnels, manage the Facebook ads, etc...?

That's what led to the second company: **Kaifect**, which is a full service marketing agency. Working with Kaifect allows you to focus on what you do best, while we take care of the rest.

In very simple terms:

We work with authors, speakers, coaches, artists, trainers, business owners, and entrepreneurs to scale their knowledge and expertise, and share their message and talents with the world.

We do this by helping them create products and online courses, book more speaking engagements, negotiate more lucrative contracts, and move towards the lifestyle they desire.

When I say full-service, I mean full-service. The Kaifect

agency builds websites, helps clients become more active on social media, grows email lists of subscribers who are interested in their content. We work closely with clients to create content (such as blogs, vlogs, podcasts) and then we help them to see what content is most popular and use that data to create and launch products, books, online courses, or other types of products. We optimize their marketing and sales funnels and then fill that funnel with both organic and paid traffic.

In other words, **we build a Machine for each of our clients!**

When clients work with us, they typically start to receive more inquiries for private coaching, keynote speaking, or whatever specific services they are offering. When that happens, we represent them and manage the process from A to Z so that **the client is able to focus on what they do best** (speaking, coaching, managing their business) while **we handle the rest** (marketing, negotiation, booking, follow up, etc…).

Within a few months of working together, our clients typically have a Machine in place that generates new leads, sells more products, and gets more speaking/consulting inquiries around the clock. **It becomes this crazy, awesome cycle.**

GENERATE NEW LEADS

ACQUIRE REFERRALS

SELL MORE PRODUCTS

GET NEW CLIENTS

Demand is higher than ever and we are ultra focused on delivering life-changing results for our clients.

Why is demand increasing even though we are not actively marketing for new clients (and have a waiting list)?

It's because this is real.

It's not just another 'online marketing fad' or shiny new object.

The MoMachine works.

It's fun.

You'll be seen as a pro.

You'll create limitless opportunities for yourself and your family that you would have never thought possible and that's what excites me so much about this.

In addition to being a business owner and entrepreneur, I also work with select clients as a...

2) Business & Marketing Coach

I work with business owners on improving their systems, processes, sales, and online marketing. Much of my work is dedicated to helping authors, speakers, coaches, entrepreneurs, thought leaders, and business owners do 2 things:

1. Create Value

2. Capture Attention

At its very core, that is what we're doing within the Machine.

Why do I love helping people create, package, and promote books, online courses, speaking engagements, and coaching programs?

Books, courses, speakers, and coaches have made a tremendous impact on my life, and I know how powerful they can be if you take action on what you learn. As a result, I've become obsessed with how to do this at the highest level possible.

Along the way, I've realized that **most people let fear and uncertainty prevent them from taking action…** which holds them back from getting what it is that they really want.

I have also realized that **every successful entrepreneur has a coach** (or several coaches) who helps keep them moving forward, advises them when they have tough decisions to make, and inspires them with fresh ideas and perspectives to grow their business.

Without advertising this, I started to receive an overwhelming demand from business owners, athletic departments, and corporate organizations who already have a marketing & sales team in place, but are looking to get 1% better and wanted me to be available in an advisor/coaching role.

After installing The Machine and starting to work with a few clients who had an 'agent', they inquired about having me represent them in their speaking, coaching, book deals, etc... It was a very natural fit and I had great relationships with them, so it only made sense to expand and develop the skills necessary to also represent them as their...

3) Agent

This is limited to an exclusive group of coaches, athletes, artists, authors, and speakers that I not only work with to **negotiate contracts, book speaking engagements,** and **coordinate appearances,** but also to build their brand and maximize their impact, regardless of the arena that they compete in.

In essence, what we've done is flip the agency model to focus on what is truly important to the client (both now and in the future).

The same principles used in The MoMachine (online marketing and personal branding) are also used as the pillars to position our clients and create additional revenue streams.

4) Author & Speaker

As a result of the above, I also write, speak, and share my experiences with people like yourself in an effort to help you shorten your learning curve.

I've also found that creating content (and writing this book) has allowed me to experience much of what our clients experience on a regular basis.

The development of my personal brand has also given me the opportunity to experiment with various ideas, strategies, and concepts. (I'd much rather be the 'guinea pig' and report back to you with real data and proven results than to ask you to try something I've never done before.)

The best thing about wearing these 4 hats: No 2 days are ever the same and I feel like **I am very closely aligned with my calling, doing the work that I was put here to do.**

Enough about me. Let's get started…

The 3 Phases of Building Your Online Business

Over the years, I've seen that every client or individual who comes to us is in 1 of these 3 Phases (and you can probably quickly identify which phase you are in)... There are both challenges and advantages to being in each phase which are outlined below:

Phase 0

Phase Zero is the client who has an idea, knowledge, expertise, and/or experiences that they want to share with the world (or a great new business idea), and **they haven't started yet.**

Advantages of Phase 0:

- You have the ability to decide and get clear on your message that you want to share with the world.

- You have time to identify your passions, your strengths, and what it is that you really love to do before you get started.

- You still have the opportunity to identify and talk to other leaders in the industry about the feasibility of your ideas.

- You aren't tied down to restricting publishing commitments that prevent you from having the freedom and control you desire.

- By understanding how the Machine fits together before you get started, you will have a much clearer picture on what order and which things you need to focus on (and which you don't) to have the greatest chance of success.

Challenges of Phase 0:

- There are so many directions that you can go. Sometimes it can be difficult to choose one or to pick a niche that you are going to serve.

- When you understand the Machine and how much fun it can be, you'll immediately want to be in Phase 2 or 3. You must be patient in order to maximize the process and ensure that you are maintaining quality and over-delivering every step of the way in order for this Machine to work once you get to Phase 2 and 3.

Phase 1

This client has already **started to build an online presence**. They have an audience of some sort (email subscribers and/or social media followers) and they are looking to figure out how to monetize their knowledge, experience, and expertise.

Advantages of Phase 1:

- You can start putting content out there to the world today and get feedback immediately. (This will let you know what they want and what you have to give them before you create your product.)

- You already have an audience, but you've never sold them anything... so you've built up a lot of reciprocity and can continue to do so all the way through the process of building out the Machine. In other words, you've never asked them to do anything.

[There's this constant equity that builds up over the course of your business. When you provide great content and great value, you're making a deposit. When you ask for something, you're making a withdrawal, and you've got to constantly balance that to make sure that you are providing value in the right way.]

- If you're in Phase 1, you've made many deposits and have yet to make a withdrawal. That's a great place to be.

Challenges of Phase 1:

- You've already got an audience and you want to make sure that you serve them in the right way... This can make picking which product and services that you really want to get behind more difficult.

Phase 2

If you've established your presence, have an audience that you communicate with on a regular basis, and **have products/services that you're actively marketing**, you are in Phase 2.

Advantages of Phase 2:

- You are so close to breaking through and to having all the gears of the Machine turning for you.

- You've probably got a ton of great content that you can share with your audience.

- If you've already written a book(s), perhaps you didn't launch them in the way that they deserve to be launched, so you can go back and leverage much of that content that you've already written or recorded, and start to share that with your audience immediately.

NOTE: There is probably someone that you know who could help you curate the content that you've already created. That can then be scheduled out as several months worth of social media content or blog posts, which can then be emailed to your subscribers as a way to build up good will before you implement other components of the Machine.

- Your presence online or your website probably only needs a few tweaks to really get to the next level in terms of reaching more people, selling more products, getting booked for more speaking engagements, and/or acquiring more clients.

Challenges of Phase 2:

- You might have already promoted a specific product over and over to your list, so you're going to have to get creative if you want to relaunch that product.

- If you've already written a book, maybe you can take that to the next level by adding a deluxe video or audio program around that same content that goes deeper.

Phase 3

This is the client who is rocking and rolling. They have a solid foundation, great content, **products and services that are selling every day, marketing funnels in place and are actively filling those funnels with paid advertising.** They're in a position to scale (or have already scaled) their business. It's very organized and optimized. They're focused on overdelivering their front end product or service with the Machine in place on the backend. They know exactly where to focus their time and energy to produce the greatest returns.

Advantages of Phase 3:

- You've got it going. You've got a lot already in place with regards to the Machine.

- You've already got a lot of numbers in your business that maybe you're not tracking or haven't organized yet, but when you go back and look at these numbers and these statistics, you'll immediately know where your opportunities lie.

- You're probably very close to making a couple small

tweaks and seeing a massive difference in your results.

- You've got multiple avenues and angles you can take on building out multiple funnels with your products and services.

Challenges of Phase 3:

- You might have been doing this for a long time and the landscape is changing rapidly. It's very important that you take time to step back from your business and look at what is being done, what's working, and how you can innovate, how you can take your existing business to another level (by using what's inside this book).

- Some entrepreneurs in Phase 3 can quickly become complacent, which usually results in them becoming 'bored' with their work and less motivated to keep pushing forward.

When a client approaches us, we identify what phase they are in. We get clear on where they're at. Then, we look at what they need to do moving forward to get to the next level.

NOTE: It's important to move through the phases sequentially. If you try to jump from Phase 0 to Phase 3, you will miss some critical ingredients to a well-oiled

Machine.

If a client is in Phase 0, we work relentlessly to get them into Phase 1 as soon as possible. If they're in Phase 1, our goal is to get them to Phase 2. If they're in Phase 2, our goal is to move them to Phase 3.

What's In This For Me?

If you're an expert, an author, a speaker, a coach, a consultant, a business owner, an entrepreneur, a network marketer... **the MoMachine will work for you.**

I've now helped over 100 clients, entrepreneurs, authors, speakers, and coaches build wildly profitable online businesses by:

- organizing their business,
- streamlining their message,
- generating more leads,
- selling more products,
- booking more speaking engagements,
- getting more clients,
- maximizing their impact, and
- creating or increasing existing revenue streams.

Whether you're a startup author or speaker who hasn't written or published a book yet, or if you already have an established audience, this is the proven system that is going to take you to the next level.

What's crazy is:

I probably won't teach you or show you anything in this book that you haven't heard before. It's the <u>sequence</u> and <u>layering</u> that makes this so powerful.

The MoMachine has helped clients pay for their kid's college tuition.

It's helped clients quit their 9-5 job.

It's helped corporate executives make additional income and start to enjoy the work that they're doing.

The MoMachine has helped retired coaches get back in the game and be able to do what they love most.

I've tested all the different methods that the gurus are teaching and through that, I've done a lot of things wrong. I've also done a lot of things right and have been able to see trends that will help you.

I'm a big believer in taking **action.**

In this book, we're going to shorten your learning curve and give you exactly what you need to do – nothing more, nothing less.

You can think of this as the cheat sheet.

The MoMachine is a simplified system you can use to get paid what you're worth for helping lots of people.

And, this works for anyone…

If you're just getting started, The Machine is the <u>only</u> thing that you need to focus on. Once you move into Phase 1, stay there for at least 60-90 days.

If you want to **build your brand on YouTube**, create videos, build an audience and then get paid through advertising, you need to integrate The Machine.

If you have a **book idea** in your head and you don't know what's next, you need to move through these phases of The Machine to make sure that your book gets written, launched, sold, and promoted in the way that it deserves.

Many entrepreneurs or potential authors or speakers are concerned with coming off as self-promotional. The Machine allows you to do this in a way that is organic and **not self-promotional**. It is a natural sequence that brings people into your world, educates them, gives them great value, and if they want more, they have the opportunity to take the next step.

It's not self-promotional because when you look at the end game, you're targeting exactly the people that you want to reach and giving them value. **If they want more, they will have the opportunity to invest in your products and services.** If they don't, they won't. So in no way do you personally need to constantly be posting and promoting your own products and services.

What's also really cool about creating The Machine is that once you have it in place, you know exactly who's following you, you know exactly what they want, and that gives you tremendous input into what you can create next. (You'll learn more about this in a bit...)

You might be reading this and thinking, **"All I really want is more speaking engagements."** Well, one of the best ways to get more speaking engagements is to put this Machine in place.

If you just don't feel like there's enough people **consuming the content** that you're putting out there, you need to get The Machine in place as soon as possible. Traffic is not the problem. It never has been.

If you put The Machine to work for you, everything will start to fit together.

Soon, it will all make sense and all the work that you've put in will start to come to fruition.

If you've started to create content and you've written a book but now you're not sure what's next... keep reading! :) Even if you've already released your book, you can still **relaunch your book**. Even though it might have been written a year or two ago, I'm sure it still provides great value (and probably has some great reviews and social proof you can leverage now).

If you've already got a book that you launched and **sales have dropped off**, you need to put a Machine in place that continues to sell your products all day, every day. That's only possible through The Machine.

If your core business is **subscription or membership-based**, The Machine is the only way that you are going to grow and scale your membership. You need some level of content being put out there for free and then you need a premium version of your content. You have to launch your membership. You have to have a funnel that leads people into your membership and you should be using Facebook advertising to continually drive traffic into your funnel. Without paid advertising, it's basically up to you to continually drive organic traffic manually through posting and emailing and telling people about yourself. Once you put the Part 8 of The Machine in place, you'll have new members joining every single day.

If you've got an **established business** or have a lot of other things going on, but deep down you know that you really want to focus on building your personal brand, you need to have a Machine in place to do so. The beautiful thing about The Machine is that it will tell you exactly what's working, and where your time and energy is best focused to maximize the results and the impact of The Machine.

If you have a **non-profit**, the best way to raise more money and be able to make a bigger impact in the world is through building this Machine for your non-profit organization. You need a website. You need an email list of your core raving fans. You have to be active on social media, sharing the impact that your organization is making. You have to launch your non-profit organization because you have to show up with momentum. Once you have that in place, you should be driving traffic to your mission. That is the only way you will scale your non-profit organization to make a massive difference in the world.

If you're concerned about **legacy**, The Machine gives you a great way to make sure that your information, your teachings, your content, will be available and consumed for the rest of time, even beyond your lifetime.

If you're making 6+ figures per year through your online business, you probably have several of these components of The Machine in place. You've probably launched your products. You've probably got funnels driving people to your products. You've probably got some sort of advertising and organic traffic that's constantly filling the funnel. You still need to look at **tracking all components of this Machine** very closely, organizing, optimizing, and ensuring that you're over-delivering in every step of the process. (I'll show you how to do that in a minute.)

If you take a step back and look at your business, and you look at every component of this Machine like we do, I guarantee that you will see opportunities to tighten up some loose nuts and bolts that will make a big difference in your results.

Don't ever discount what having another set of eyes on your work can bring to the table. **Some of the real breakthroughs in my business have come as a result of asking for help.**

2 Critical Things to Focus On

So You Don't Get Frustrated or Burned Out

There are two things that I really love to do:

Simplify and Maximize.

Doing this will help keep you focused and energized. When things get complex, it's easy to shut down. When you know there are opportunities that you're not taking advantage of, it's hard to focus on bringing your best self to this moment.

When you have The Machine in place, you'll know that nothing will fall through the cracks.

It's very simple.

Eliminate the noise.

Simplify your focus: Create value. Capture attention.

(REMEMBER: Simple does <u>not</u> mean easy.)

It will give you the best chance to maximize your opportunities.

Maximize your impact.

Maximize your income.

This gives yourself the best chance for success with the knowledge and the expertise that you already have.

I know you've got a lot going on. You've got a busy schedule and I'm grateful that you're reading this because I know how powerful and life-changing this can be for you.

To get the most out of this book:

- Turn off your notifications.

- Get out of your inbox.

- Turn off the TV.

- Get out your notepad.

The 3 Myths of Online Marketing

Myth #1: You need to be an 'expert'.

You don't have to be an expert to get started but you do need to take action and get started to be an expert.

I've worked with clients who had zero previous experience, that didn't understand any of the lingo, and I've helped them create more than six figures in online revenue each year. You have what it takes.

Myth #2: You have to become a self promoter.

With the MoMachine, you'll see exactly how you can help a ton of people and reach a much larger audience than you are right now with your message, without being perceived as self promotional.

You might be nervous and I get that. This might be new territory for you. I've been there. We've all been there.

The bottom line is: **If you can help others, you need to help them.** Sometimes that requires that we get out of our comfort zone but isn't that what we're here to do?

Myth #3: You need a big list or an audience.

Traffic, or getting people into your world, is not a problem and it never has been. You'll hear a lot of people talking about how they struggle to get traffic. They built a website and no one comes. Traffic is not a problem and it never has been. You're about to see exactly why.

Disclaimer

If you want to get rich quick, or you're not prepared to put in the work, or you're not truly passionate about helping people, **this is <u>not</u> for you.**

But if you're ready to make moves, if you're ready to get after it, if you want to start maximizing opportunities and stop letting things fall through the cracks, **this <u>is</u> for you.**

There are many people out there who may have more experience and have been doing this longer than we have, but The MoMachine will help you understand how everything fits together in order to have more clarity moving forward.

There is more than one way to do things. This relates to everything in life, but specifically online marketing and your business. You need to find what works for you, which is what I'm about to show you *how* to do. You're going to see what's available, how it all fits together, and then test what works for you.

The MoMachine has been proven to produce amazing results for myself and for our clients, their businesses, and their families.

As long as you keep your focus on impact and helping people, this will work for you.

The MoMachine

This is a proven system to maximize your impact and your income without any of the chaos and confusion that the gurus are throwing around.

PLUS: You'll be able to understand this even if you have little to no knowledge or expertise with technology or online marketing.

From studying hours and hours of books, online courses, attending events, I've tested and tried everything that's out there to see what works and what doesn't. I've ultimately drilled it down to what is now referred to as The MoMachine.

Before we jump in to these 8 important components of The MoMachine, I want to make something very clear:

Everything that you do inside your Machine will have a purpose and be done with intent.

There's detailed tracking and analytics in place for you to track your process and your system to know exactly where your time and energy needs to be focused.

There are different components of the Machine that are more effective for some clients than others, but it's important for you to understand them all.

One of the keys to moving from Phase 0 to 1, from 1 to 2, and from 2 to 3 is by understanding The Machine, where you're at, what your strengths and weaknesses are, and what you need to do to get all of the pieces in place to make sure everything works together nicely.

Impact > Income

Keeping the impact greater than the income is <u>essential</u> through this entire process. If you focus on income, you will probably make less income… but if you focus on **impact, serving, giving, and helping others**, the income will be there as a byproduct of delivering great value.

Let's Go!

Building a well-oiled Machine begins with a simple, clean, professional…

#1) Website

The first component of the MoMachine is your website. The website serves as the hub for everything that you do. It's where you'll send people to learn more about you, consume the content you create, purchase your products, etc... There are many places you can try to start but I think it is critical to begin with a quality website that clearly and efficiently communicates:

- who you are,
- what you do, and
- how you can help the visitors that come to your website.

Ideally this is done 'above the fold', which means before a user has to scroll.

Web design is one component of what we do, but a very integral one for anyone who wants to create content, sell products or services, build marketing funnels, etc…

Whether you're just getting started and want to build your site from scratch, or a business owner who just wants to make basic updates, add blog posts, etc…, it's important that you understand these fundamental concepts and be certain that your website is aligned with your mission.

The internet is evolving very quickly and with that, the high-level concepts and strategies remain the same, but the tactics, tools, and techniques are changing rapidly.

Although I wouldn't consider myself a 'web developer', here are a few **important lessons I've learned from building over 100 websites in the past 5 years…**

1) There are many different ways to build a website.

The purpose of each is unique. It is important that the brand is visually consistent across all platforms (web, social, etc…) so that plays a large role in the process. There are 2 things I always do before beginning construction: framework the page structure -and- build a cohesive brand guide that includes the logo, colors, fonts, etc…

2) A website is simply a tool to educate your audience and engage with them.

Some people ask if they even need a website anymore with the growing popularity of social media. I wouldn't say that every person has to have a website, but even if you only represent a personal brand, there are many advantages to having a website, such as streamlining your process for handling inquiries on speaking engagements, public appearances, sponsorship opportunities, etc…

IMPORTANT: If you want to sell a product (digital or physical), I highly recommend having a website that serves as the hub, that you then use social media, e-mail, and paid advertising to drive traffic to.

3) If you're serious about impacting others on a larger scale, you should have a website.

Even if you don't have a product/service and don't plan on ever creating/offering one, a website gives you a platform to create content, upload videos, host a podcast, etc… In short, your website is where you create value to give your tribe.

4) Creating a world class website takes longer than you anticipate.

Just like putting this book together, building, designing, optimizing and testing different elements of a website take time. If you want to build your own website, I highly suggest you see the **MoTools** section at the end of this book and also give yourself 2-3x more time than you expect it will take. (I've invested years into doing this, making countless mistakes, staying up all night to get things fixed, and hope that this book, along with the **MoTools**, will shorten your learning curve and get you up and running with fewer obstacles.)

5) Technology is evolving quickly, and with that, so are the capabilities of a website.

10 years ago, almost all visits to a website were from a computer. As of 2018, more than 75% of all website traffic that we are tracking analytics on is coming from users on a mobile device. From a web design perspective, that means your site should be built for mobile first, then desktop…

6) There is a consistent sequence that cold traffic goes through.

When a new user arrives at your website, it's like meeting a new friend. You then grab their attention by introducing yourself. The more value you can provide upfront, the faster you will build the trust that is necessary for them to want to do business with you. Once you've built that relationship, you can begin to exchange value (or make a sale).

Your website needs to accommodate them regardless of which stage they're in. You can utilize e-mail autoresponders (which we'll discuss later on) as well to build the relationship after they've visited your site and/or subscribed to your list.

Be patient with the process, but trust it… It's worth the time and energy to **build the platform that allows you to pursue your passions.**

MoTip: Have a 'lead magnet' on your homepage. You may have heard of this or you may already be collecting leads using one… You've also probably opted in for other lead magnets before (i.e. the 10% off if you give us your e-mail address, free downloadable report, etc…).

Essentially **you're giving away something of value in**

exchange for their email address. This can be something that you feel could almost be a product, something that you could charge money for, but in this case you're using it to bring someone into your world, give them value, create a quick win, and then develop that relationship.

A lead magnet could be anything from a PDF to a video series to a particular audio or report. There are a lot of different types of lead magnets but what's most important here is that you give people a reason to visit your site and are making sure that it serves a purpose. You're building your email list and they're getting real value from you.

We're on a mission to keep getting 1% better every day and are always open to suggestions, ideas, and feedback that you have... If you ever come across a website that we've built and see something we could test or improve, please send an email to **Kaizen@Kaifect.com** (our improvement/tip line). We'd love to hear from you!

Once you have your website up and running, you'll want to quickly start using...

#2) Email

Many people say that email marketing is dead.

I can promise you that is <u>not</u> true.

NOTE: There is a big difference between emailing value to a list of qualified subscribers and sending spam that no one ever asked for.

Email is still more effective and more powerful when it comes to getting a direct response to an offer that you make or to a piece of content that you want someone to read, watch, or listen to.

As an entrepreneur, author, speaker, or coach, you need to <u>always</u> be building your email list. There are many ways to build the email list, which we will get into, but it is the core asset that you have in this business.

You <u>don't</u> own your Twitter followers or Facebook Page Likes. You <u>do</u> own your e-mail list.

If you want:

- more traffic to your website
- more people to read your blogs
- more people to watch your videos
- more people to listen to your podcast
- more product sales
- more 1-on-1 coaching clients
- more speaking engagements
- more impact
- more legacy
- to help more people
- to have more fun

…then you need to be building your e-mail list!

(If you do it right, it's like having a license to print money!)

You want to use email to keep your 'raving fans' up to date on your latest and greatest material. I say that because ultimately your most loyal followers are going to be subscribers to your email list. They're going to opt in for what you have to give them, so make sure that you use email to keep them up to date on what you're doing and how they can get involved.

So, how do you create and build your e-mail list?

There are many online software options available now that make this very simple for you. If you're just getting started, MailChimp is a great option (and is free up to 2,000 subscribers).

Within each of these is typically a few different main tools to use:

Lists are the subscribers that can be segmented into groups so that you can mail them accordingly. (You should have separate lists of prospects and customers, so that you know who has bought something from you and who hasn't.) The more information you have from your subscribers, the better. This allows you to message them accordingly.

Campaigns are the automated e-mail sequences that you can setup for subscribers to go through.

Broadcasts give you the ability to write a one-off e-mail and send it to your list.

Once you have your e-mail software setup, it is time to start building your list...

For starters, create a high value Lead Magnet.

You've seen these everywhere on the web... Why? Because they work.

In essence, you need to think through:

- What type of people are you trying to attract?
- What do you have that they want?
- What problem can you help them solve?

Now, what type of 'lead magnet' can you put together and deliver electronically to them instantly after they opt-in?

These could include:

- PDFs (eBook, one-page report, charts)
- Audios/Videos (maybe an excerpt from a product you've created)
- Checklists (people love checklists!)
- Templates (these convert really well)
- Exclusive Discounts (effective in eCommerce businesses)

Once you've got your e-mail software setup and your

lead magnet on your website, you can explore a variety of ways to drive traffic (which we will cover later in the Machine)...

Make sure you are consciously making an effort to move your social media 'followers' to your e-mail list.

Once you have a list, here are 5 practical applications for you to use e-mail for:

1) Give Value and Teach

The most effective way I've seen to build a relationship with your tribe is to give them real value consistently over time that helps them solve problems, improve their life/business, and generate quick wins. A value-first content strategy is arguably the fastest way to build your e-mail list.

2) Notifying of a New Blog Post, Podcast, or Video on your Website

This goes with the value-first content strategy... If you create a new blog post or record a new podcast, you can't assume all of your people will find it on your site. It is your responsibility (if you believe in your work) to let them know. **E-mail is the most reliable, direct form of communication to do this.** (I highly recommend you also post on social media, and repurpose some of your best content there also, but don't forget to e-mail!)

3) Amplify a Social Media Post

When you hit it big on social with a popular post, why not pour gasoline on the fire by e-mailing your list with a link to the post? (I'd recommend adding some additional context to the e-mail so your subscribers receive additional value… a common theme that you should be following!)

4) Sell Your Product/Service

If you have a product that can improve someone's life, you owe it to them to do everything possible to tell them about it. E-mail allows you to tell a story around the product/service and then provide a call to action (CTA) linking them to your website if they want to learn more. (Don't try to sell them on every product and service you offer at once. Maintain a singular focus and explain the benefits they will experience as a result of your product!)

5) Build Your Relationship

Very much like when you meet someone in person, they don't necessarily want to hear your life story immediately. When someone opts in to your e-mail list, make it your mission to give them value and help create a meaningful win ASAP. This can be done with autoresponder sequences that are triggered immediately when they opt-in, 1 day after, 3 days after, etc…

That first e-mail that is sent can include a quick welcome as well as a link to download whatever it is that they opted in for. The follow-up e-mails can include additional information, FAQs, and eventually lead them (if you've built up enough reciprocity) to pursue working with you, buy your product, ask to schedule a strategy session, join your membership, etc…

Your readers should feel as if they have a personal connection with you. That is what gets them to open, read, click, etc...

Lastly, before writing/sending, ask yourself what the desired outcome of the e-mail is…

Don't forget to provide the desired CTA (call-to-action) within the e-mail for the reader to take the next step.

The CTA can range from clicking the link to read the rest of your blog post, to clicking through to watch your most recent Facebook Live broadcast that has stacked up some serious social love, to enrolling in your new course, or to getting a ticket to your next event...

Once you start mailing your list, you can track a number of analytics of each broadcast/campaign... Most important of those are the Open Rate (largely dictated by your existing relationship and subject line), and the Click Through Rate (how many readers clicked a link in your e-mail).

To quickly recap:

- Always be building your e-mail list.
- Create a lead magnet to give people a reason to join.
- Track your conversion rates and find what is most effective for you.
- Move social media followers to your e-mail list.
- Give value.
- Make it about them.

- Be real.

- Maintain great tempo.

- If you have a product/service that can improve their life, tell them about it!

MoTip: Utilize an autoresponder sequence to welcome new subscribers into your world.

We talked about your 'lead magnet'. Let's say you are giving them a 7-page PDF report. After they opt in, your autoresponder sequence is going to email them a link to download that PDF and then you can put an automated sequence together after that giving them access to your most popular posts, podcasts, etc… for 3-7 days following. Make sure that you're using that to build the relationship and educate them on who you are and what you do.

It doesn't need to be some crazy 30 day sales sequence. Keep it simple. Give value.

Once you've got your e-mail list setup and understand how you are going to use it, then we can start to focus on…

#3) Social

When it comes to capturing attention, social media is one of the best ways to do it.

You've got your website as the hub, then you have your email list, and then social media, which you're using to move people to your email list. You're ultimately moving people from being followers on Instagram, Twitter, Facebook to being subscribers of your email list.

With that being said, you can still promote your products and services and your content directly on social media, not only to your email list, but they work together nicely and they really feed off of one another so **it is ultra important that you are active on social media**, that you have a presence, and that you're posting regularly.

Social media is changing very quickly, but to keep your Machine moving, you've got to understand how it works and be sure you at least have accounts on pertinent platforms.

IMO: Social media is about building your network and strengthening relationships with direct engagement.

I often talk about the importance of identifying your avatar and building a relationship with them. That includes knowing where they spend time, which leads into my first observation...

If you're not sure about all this social media stuff, now is probably a good time to start looking into it.

When it comes to reaching and helping more people, it is critical that you are where they are. Think about your ideal avatar (the one person that you can help the most)... Do they use social media? How often? Facebook? Instagram? Twitter?

When consulting with collegiate athletic departments/teams on the recruiting (and brand building) process, I frequently discuss the importance of having a presence on recruits' favorite platforms... When a coach gets off their first phone call with a recruit, what do you think the recruit is going to do next?

Throughout my work with prospective student-athletes, the response is overwhelming that they're headed to their favorite social media platform (Instagram, if we're talking about Millennials) and searching for the coach's name to learn more about them.

If you "only use Twitter" and they don't find you on Instagram, hopefully they check Twitter, but more than likely they're on to the next…

But, if they do find your profile and can learn more about what's important to you, what your program represents, etc… you've now developed a deeper relationship with the recruit you just spoke with, and that rapport can go a long way in the recruiting process when you are talking with numerous recruits.

I recommend at least having a presence on Facebook, Twitter, Instagram, and LinkedIn.

Each platform has a unique purpose. Use it accordingly.

With Twitter's 280-character limit on text (and 2:20 limit on videos), the platform is created to share short bits of information. You can also include links in your Tweets to your website if you want to provide more than is permitted. The Retweet feature makes shareability a factor in creating content. More on that in a bit…

Facebook is created for more long-form text and has much higher limits on the length of videos. Facebook has Profiles, Pages, and Groups. (You'll need a Profile to use Facebook and a Page to run Facebook Ads. Groups are a great way to create a community around one central purpose or mission.)

Instagram is a primarily visual platform with each post requiring at least one photo or video (up to 1 minute)..

The Instagram Story feature is similar to what Snapchat was… up to 15 second (vertical) videos, or photos that provide users with a more in-depth, raw, unedited look into your life.

LinkedIn is a more professional platform used for networking.

YouTube is a video platform that has recently increased its social features, but at least serves as a great place to host your videos (for free).

If you have the resources available (time or team) to do so, make an effort to post natively to each platform… meaning that if you have a photo you'd like to post to each platform, don't connect all your accounts to Instagram so that Twitter & Facebook auto-post an IG link. To me, it looks lazy.

Don't be romantic about the platform.

While each platform does have a unique purpose, don't become too attached to any one in particular as their features are changing rapidly. Remember that you don't own anything on social media and it could all be taken away from you very quickly. Therefore, you don't want to become dependent on any one single platform. (That is why building your e-mail list is so important!)

Is this something my avatar would want to share with their followers?

Depending on the desired outcome, this is a question to ask yourself before posting:

Why do some posts go 'viral'?

They contain a high level of shareability…

For instance: If you're an author who has a large number of sport coaches following you, think about if what you are about to post is something they would want to share with their players… In many cases, coaches decide what to post (or share) based on if they think their followers would find value in it.

Additionally, there are tremendous insights and analytics available now on all of the popular social media platforms that allow you to see what days and times people are engaging with your content.

Many people ask when to post. There are a few general rules of thumb, but I am a big fan of testing and basing those decisions off of data that tells you exactly when your followers are most active.

As you are working to build authority, something else to keep in mind when creating content is:

Scroll Stopping

Is there a creative, unique element you can add to your post to stop users from scrolling right over what you just worked so hard to create?

Before attaching an image or video to a post, ask yourself: Is this scroll stopping?

Use social media for what it was created to be used for.

Now, of course there are times when you are going to be promoting a product or service, but social media should be used to communicate and have meaningful conversations.

Replying to (or at least acknowledging) your followers' comments can go a long way.

As a general rule of thumb, you should be adding value ~80%, sharing other content ~10%, and promoting/selling ~10%.

While others are panicking about Facebook's algorithm changes, I think it is a great move to increase the amount of real interaction happening among the people and businesses you follow on Facebook. It will force hyperactive marketers to reconsider their plan of attack.

Have fun with it!

Be creative.

Inspire.

Share your journey.

Try new things.

See what works and what your people like.

Turn off your notifications and schedule time each day to check in on your accounts.

If you want to be more productive and have greater impact, you can't allow every like or comment to distract you from what you're focused on. You can also turn off the little red 'badges' so you're not tempted to check in on your social media apps all day long.

If you're not intentional about how you use social media, it will end up using you.

(You know... That black hole you fall into and come out of 15 minutes later wondering what just happened!)

The smartphone has trained us to immediately respond to any alert or notification. We must break this habit and be more intentional with our time and energy.

Use direct messages for customer support.

If your prospects or customers want to inquire about products/services via direct messages or Facebook Messenger, you should have a system in place to reply to them within 24 hours. Having a built-in contact form on your website will reduce these, but if your customer wants to talk with you on a platform they are comfortable with, then reply to them there, or have someone who is able to do that for you. Responsiveness is key!

Do more live video broadcasts.

Technology makes it very simple now to go live for all of your followers anytime, anywhere. Facebook and Instagram allow you to do this in-app, but there are tools like BeLive.TV and Zoom that provide awesome features to take your live broadcasts to the next level.

If you don't feel like you can keep up, automate.

There are several social media management apps available now that allow you to schedule your social media posts at a specific date and time in the future. If you're struggling with constant FOMO on social, start by automating a few posts on Facebook or Twitter. Don't let it become more than 50% of your posts as there is true power in real-time interaction, but if you have scheduled or recurring events that you know are going to require posting to social media, then try automating them so can direct your focus where it needs to be.

Don't expect all of your followers to see everything you post.

(I saved this for last because I think it is most important.)

Maybe this was the case 5-10 years ago, but not anymore. There are so many people fighting for the attention of your audience that you can never assume that if you post something your followers will see it.

The algorithms are constantly changing and the most popular posts (hopefully yours) are moving towards the top of your feed. Attention spans are shortening. Time spent in-app is decreasing, while frequency is increasing…

Bottom line is that if you feel strongly about something or want to promote products/services, you should be willing to pay for the attention of your target market.

The Facebook Ad platform is possibly the most robust marketing tool I've ever seen (and it keeps getting better).

Advertising on social media can be very complex, but profitable if you trust the process. (We'll talk more about this later on…)

If you want to share your message with the world, use social media.

There is a learning curve involved, but it is worth it (and I'd love to help).

Have a presence on all popular platforms. Focus on your strengths.

Post more frequently. Use more video. Try a live broadcast.

Automate when needed.

Ask yourself about the shareability before posting.

Turn off notifications. Check in once per day.

Enjoy the process and have fun with it!

MoTip: Use images and videos to increase engagement. Whether it's Twitter, Facebook, Instagram, or LinkedIn, images and videos are going to increase the engagement of your post by ~50%. It may take a little more work to create these and build your library of images and videos (which we'll go into a little bit later on) but that is going to make your posts much more effective.

Also, taking the time to respond to DMs (direct messages) is a great way to create raving fans. You're creating a connection that I believe is critically important in this whole thing.

If you've got the social media thing down, it's time to go next level with your…

#4) Content

Regardless of the industry that you're in, you need to be creating content of some form. I like to take a hybrid approach to creating content in that we cover all three mediums:

- Written Text
- Audio
- Video

Everyone learns differently. Some people prefer to read. Some people prefer to listen. Some people prefer to watch. Some people want to read a physical book. Some people want to listen to an audiobook in the car. Some people want to watch a video on their computer or stream their computer to their TV and learn that way.

Regardless, I think it's important that you're creating content in all three mediums. A blog on your website is a great way to start to create content and to get feedback on what's most popular, which will help us out in the next part of the Machine...

REMEMBER: A blog on your website does not have to be just text. You can embed videos, audios, pictures, and graphics. Don't think of a blog as just strictly text.

Ultimately, I would encourage you to begin by creating all 3 types of content and seeing what your audience really resonates with. You might be great with written word. You might be great on camera and you may not be so great on recording audio. You may be great with audio and not enjoy being on camera. With that being said, video is very, very effective today in terms of building trust with another human being. **Eye contact is an important piece to building trust, and that can't be done with audio or text.**

MoTip: Identify your avatar. (Who are you writing to? Who is reading that blog post on the other end?) Then just get started writing. If it's an audio or a video, you still may want to create an outline or a script or a framework for that piece of content... but just get started!

If you're not 100% clear on who that avatar is yet, get the words on paper. The beautiful thing about content (whether it's a blog, podcast, a video) is that it gives you the ability to capture your ideas and turn them into content so fast relative to what it used to be 5-10 years ago.

Today, if you have an idea you can sit down, write the blog post, publish it, and then it goes through this Machine we're building. You email it out to your subscribers and you break it down into social media posts, driving all of them to your website where they consume that piece of content. You get feedback immediately from what resonates with your audience.

Creating content is one of the best ways to drill into your speaking topics, your coaching exercises, and even what can be potential...

#5) Products

Once you've started to create and share content with your audience, you will get a very good idea of which content you produce that is most popular. That gives you a great indication of what your first product might be.

If you start to create blog posts in one certain category that is 10-20x more popular than another, which is typically what we see once you start to create content in different categories, that gives you a great indication of what your first product might be.

Again, this goes back to the three mediums.

Written text could be a **book** or an **eBook**.

Audio could be an **audio program**.

Video could be **online course** with you teaching something on camera. (This is a lot easier than you may think because you can very easily turn your camera on from your computer or your phone and record high quality video... or you could even voiceover PowerPoint slides!)

There's also the possibility that you can create a video-based product, and then have that transcribed into text or stripped down to audio and provide a fully loaded online course that includes the videos, the downloadable audios, the transcriptions, and even move the transcriptions into worksheets that people can fill out as they watch the videos. The nice thing about a video course is that it typically justifies a higher price point, which will make the next 3 pieces of the Machine more effective and easy to integrate in your business.

If you're struggling to figure out what your core message should be or what your next product could be, consider...

The Stage Test

If I told you that you were going on stage in 10 minutes in front of 500 of your ideal avatars, what would you talk about? No preparation. No slides. You have to fill a 45 minute time slot.

Whatever you come up with is most likely your thing.

Now, go give that talk in front of the camera… or put together a PowerPoint presentation and record a voiceover! Then send it to Rev.com to get transcribed into text…

That gives you at least 3 quality pieces of content… the video, the audio, and the text transcript!

MoTip: Develop your most popular content (blog posts, podcast episodes) into products. Go deeper. When we start out with a new website for one of our clients, we like to have 3-4 blog posts on that site before we publish it… Of those 3-4 posts almost always there is 1 (and it's not always the one that you think it would be) that takes off and has 10-30x more interaction, engagement, link clicks, or comments than the others. That is a key indicator of what your first (or next) product might be.

Once you've got a quality product, it's time to…

#6) Launch

You need to show up with momentum. Once you've poured a ton of time and energy into creating your life's work, whether it's writing a book, recording an online video course, or any other creation, you owe it to yourself to show up with momentum, and to let the world know that you've created something. I very often see people who create products and then put it on their website and expect it to sell. That's not going to happen.

One of our clients famously said, **"The Field of Dreams approach does not work when it comes to selling products. Just because you build it does not mean that they will come."**

It is very important that you put together a well-thought-out strategic, creative, fun, exciting product launch around a product that you put a lot of time and energy into.

Jeff Walker's book, *Launch*, turned me on to many different concepts related to a product launch, but I've tested many different techniques and strategies through over 150 product launches now. There are many different ways to do it, but what's most important is that you understand once you create a product or write a book, **it is essential that you show up with momentum and let the world know what you've created.**

The core idea of a launch is creating an irresistible offer that provides unmatched value to your tribe.

An irresistible offer is something that makes your audience say "Yes, for sure. I'm in. I can't wait!" It provides unmatched value, meaning you're giving them more than they're giving you. We always want to err on a 51/49 or the 60/40 scale. Give them more than what they're giving you.

Within the product launch, there are time sensitive offers where we create scarcity, stack bonuses, and make an offer that they can't resist.

Whenever I hear the word 'launch', I get chills at the excitement, the opportunity, and the incredible amount of time and energy that goes into executing a successful product launch.

I live for it.

It's changed my life and it can change yours, too.

It's time to get you moving towards your first (or next) launch!

(If you don't have a product or an e-mail list yet, a launch might be exactly what you need! Stay with me…)

"Every successful product, business, and brand starts with a successful launch. You can't afford to show up slowly. You need momentum and cash flow, because they are the very lifeblood of every successful business."
-Jeff Walker

It doesn't matter what market you're in. You can launch in any niche.

You don't need money to get started. (Remember what I said earlier about launching while I was still a collegiate student-athlete at UAB!) A launch allows you to bootstrap to success without capital.

At its very core, a launch creates a huge amount of buzz and excitement before your product is ever released and features an incredible offer at a great price point that provides your customers with life-changing information.

NOTE: If your offer is not exciting and/or your product doesn't provide real value for customers, you must get that right before launching.

If you do it right, people become genuinely engaged in a 2-way conversation.

You're giving them great content whether they decide to buy or not.

It turns into this really cool 'marketing' event.

If you're tired of telling the same people to buy your stuff over and over, you need to launch!

Over the years, I've experimented and developed different variations of product launches, but I'm going to quickly summarize the model for you…

A Product Launch consists of 4 phases:

1) Pre-Pre-Launch

- Start building anticipation.
- Get a pulse on the market.
- Discover possible objections.
- (Make any necessary tweaks to your final offer!)

2) Pre-Launch

- Give your audience 3 pieces of high-value content over 5-12 days. (Sequencing is key!)

- Activate the mental triggers. (Authority, Social Proof, Anticipation, and Reciprocity are the strongest.)

- Content can vary widely, from video to audio to written PDFs (or a combination).

An easy way to think about pre-launch content is this… Remember those old-school sales letters that were 30 pages long and you probably didn't read but just scrolled to the bottom to find the price? A quality pre-launch sequence flips that long sales page on its side, delivering shorter pieces of valuable content that educate and give before you ask for the sale.

3) Launch

- Start taking orders (referred to as your 'Open Cart' period).

- This is a short, specified period of time (usually 1-7 days).

4) Post-Launch

- Follow-up with new clients who bought.

- Follow-up with new prospects who didn't buy.

- Deliver value and build your brand.

- Nailing your post-launch sets up your next launch!

Those are the 4 phases of a Launch.

Now, here are the 4 different types of Launches you can execute:

The 'Seed Launch'

If you don't have a product yet, this is the Launch for you. This is where you are essentially selling a group coaching course (maybe 6-8 weeks) with weekly calls. Before and after each call, you can survey the group asking them what they want to learn more about, what questions they have, etc… The pre-pre-launch of a Seed Launch does a lot of the heavy lifting for you. They're going to get a no-brainer discount + they're going to get more of your one-on-one attention.

NOTE: If you ever see someone else doing a Seed Launch, get in there. You're going to get a lot of attention and one-on-one hands on work with the creator as they hash out what their final product consist of.

An Internal Launch

Before you move to a JV Launch, it is important that you run an Internal Launch, meaning that you are promoting your product/service to your own e-mail list and social media followers <u>without</u> the support of affiliates/partners. You need to make sure your offer converts, build up social proof of people who are using your product and getting results, and make any necessary tweaks. Once you've successfully executed an Internal Launch, then you can move on to a…

JV (Joint Venture) Launch

This is where the money is made. A JV Launch means that you have partners who are mailing their lists and telling their people about your launch. If you make a sale to someone that a partner sends your way, you payout a commission to your partner (typically 25-50%, depending on the price point of the product).

A JV partner is very similar to an Affiliate. The distinction is typically that anyone can become an affiliate and make a commission on selling your products, while a JV partner is someone who is going all out for you and whom you have/will reciprocate for by going all out for them during their next launch.

WARNING: JV Launches can be explosive in ways that change your life and business forever. There will be a line of people waiting to buy from you when you open your cart. It's important that you're properly prepared and are ready to overdeliver your influx of new customers. (Be sure you have proper resources allocated to customer support and that you've tested all sequences thoroughly.)

Don't try a JV Launch until you've done an internal launch to your list and have proven that your offer converts. The last thing you want is to have your partners go all out for you with an offer that doesn't convert. If that happens, they probably won't be promoting for you in the future.

"The bottom line is that there are a hundred ways to create value for a potential partner – and the more value you create, the more you get back."

Last, but not least, is the...

Evergreen Launch

Like an evergreen tree, this style of launch lives on forever without a specific cart open/close time. Once you've proven one of the above launch sequences to convert well, you can transition into an Evergreen Launch... This means someone can opt-in at anytime to your pre-launch sequence, receive your content via an e-mail autoresponder, creating a very natural progression into your core offer.

Here's why I get chills when I hear the word 'Launch' (and why I love helping my clients Launch)...

- Whether someone buys from you or not, you're giving them great value and training.

- It creates crazy amounts of momentum in your business!

- Every launch creates a life of its own, in a very unique (and awesome) way.

- A launch is a great way to build your e-mail list.

- It gives you a chance to create exactly what your people want, rather than your other 'hope' marketing strategies...

- The offer typically includes stacking up some really cool bonuses for a limited time, rewarding those who take action.

- If you truly believe in what you have created and know it can help people, you owe it to yourself to do everything you can to reach as many people as possible.

- I'll never forget the moment I executed my first launch and made my first sale within 60 seconds of opening the cart.

- There's a sort of magic and excitement inside a launch that is hard to replicate.

- It forces action in your prospects to make a decision: **Yes -or- No**

- Like anything you do in life, each launch that you do gets better than the previous.

- With technology evolving, launches are becoming much more interactive and dynamic...

I could go on and on... but I think you get the point.

Now is the time for you to start planning your next launch.

(What if you could pull off 2 launches every year? How would that impact your business?)

I'd love to help you make it happen..

A large percentage of the work we do within the Kaifect agency is helping authors, speakers, coaches, entrepreneurs, and consultants **package up their knowledge into the product** and then **launch!**

MoTip: Schedule your next launch now. Show up with momentum. After you create the product, the last thing you want to do is put it on your website and hope people find it.

If you created a product and you invested yourself in that product, don't let it sit there and have no one see it, no one consume it, no one read it, listen to it, or watch it. Re-Launch!

One of the downsides that people attach to product launches is that they think their income is going to spike when they launch and then drop off. **That's true.**

Many people who run large scale launches do 2 per year (i.e. April and September). Between those launches, they're focused on building their list. We want to launch when we have something that needs to be launched but we don't want to depend on that. If you depend on 1-2 launches per year and something goes wrong or one thing is off, it becomes difficult to recover and make up from that. We want to utilize the launch but we don't want to depend on them for our entire revenue.

Your income will spike with a product launch… but let's raise the basement by building out your…

#7) Funnel

A marketing funnel is a logical, efficient, and effective sequence that scales your time and energy by giving your customers what they want, when they need it, and allows you start making sales while you sleep.

DISCLAIMER: It is critical that you keep the <u>impact</u> greater than the <u>income</u> and that your focus is on helping people to improve their lives, because within the marketing funnel, you can't help but sell the products that you have created.

The marketing funnel, very simply put, is bringing a cold prospect into your world, educating them on who you are, what you do, how you can help them, and then providing solutions to the problems that they might have.

The top of the funnel starts with **free content**. What are you putting out there on social? What do you email out to your list? What type of PR campaigns are you doing? What type of media are you publishing? All of those things should be bringing people into the funnel and one of the best ways to track this is by seeing if those things are building your email list. Are people consuming your content that you put out there for free at the top of the funnel and subscribing to your email list?

Then they start to move downward through the funnel to your **low-priced products** (such as a $10-$20 book or eBook), and then come your **middle tier products** (such as a $100-$300 online course).

The bottom of your funnel could be **speaking engagements, private coaching or consulting.**

Here's what your funnel could look like:

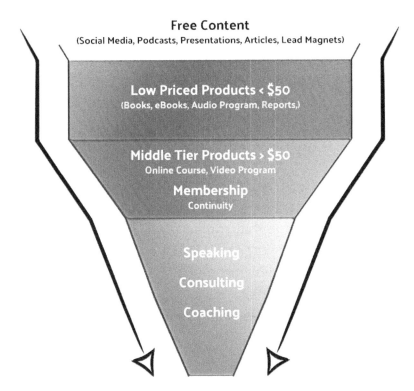

Ultimately, we want to make sure if someone comes into your world and reads your book that they say, "Wow, this is great. I learned a ton. What's next?"

We have to make sure that we have what they need next (the next solution) right there ready for them.

If they then purchase your $250 online course, go through it, and then want to bring you in to work with their organization or their team, it's up to you to provide them with the opportunity to either fill out an application or contact someone about making that happen.

Or, in another situation: If you're selling a weight loss product, pretty soon their clothes aren't going to fit anymore... How can you help them with that? (Start thinking backwards and providing solutions for your customers every step of the way.)

Too many entrepreneurs are leaving this to chance and missing out on lots of potential revenue. They publish a book and then hope that someone will like it, then come back and buy the next one, or find their private coaching, and submit an application, etc... That's not always the case. We want to make it readily available for them. **Anticipate that they are going to love your product and want more.**

MoTip: If you can get your ACV (Average Cart Value to $25-30, you're going to be able to scale pretty quickly. The most effective way to do this is to have a $97+ product at the end of your funnel that converts at 1-2%.

Your ACV can be calculated by taking your total funnel revenue divided by the number of orders.

For Example:

Today's Revenue: $10,000

Today's Number of Orders: 100

$10,000 / 100 = $100 (Average Cart Value)

So, what's next? Once your funnel has been battle tested and optimized, now we pour gas on the fire with....

#8) Advertising

You've created the value. Now it's time to capture attention.

There are hundreds of ways to advertise online. Once you have a funnel in place, you can start to fill that funnel with endless traffic from paid advertising.

By far, the most effective is **Facebook Ads**.

Facebook is so powerful that, IMO, it makes the others pretty much irrelevant. There are some businesses where Google Ads can be effective, but most likely Facebook Ads are going to be much more powerful.

Facebook also owns Instagram, so advertising on Facebook gives you the opportunity for placements on Instagram.

You can also fill the funnel with organic traffic, but a great way to get feedback on that funnel as soon as it's ready is to flip the switch on your ads and **get traffic in there to start to see how those numbers line up.**

Many entrepreneurs say that traffic is a problem. They think about writing a book or launching a new product, but they don't do it because they don't know who's going to read it.

Traffic is not a problem. It never has been, and it never will be. You just need to know:

1. where to find your people, and

2. how to get their attention!

Utilizing Facebook's advertising platform allows you to use very specific, detailed targeting methods to make sure your ad is being shown to the right people.

Here's the goal: For every $1 you give Facebook, you want to get at least $2 back.

Now if I gave you $2 every time you gave me $1, how often would you do that?

I hope you would do it all day, everyday!

That's what we're talking about here. (We even have some campaigns where we get $10-20 out for every $1 we put in!)

Want to get some of that in your business?

There are 3 basic concepts for you to understand when it comes to Facebook Advertising:

Campaigns

At the Campaign level, you are choosing your objective (generate leads, get clicks, or what we use most frequently is specific Custom Conversions). Once you choose your primary objective, Facebook will optimize your ads to what you've indicated. Trust me, Facebook wants you to win big, too! The smarter their platform is, the more money you're going to give Mr. Zuckerberg! :)

Ad Sets

Once you've got the Campaign chosen, now it's on to choose the Ad Set. This is essentially the Audience, or who you want to show your ads to.

This could be another book on its own but, based on the hundreds of thousands of dollars we've spent on Facebook, here are the 3 best Ad Sets that we use for almost every client:

- **Those Who Like Your Page and Friends of Those Who Like Your Page** (Didn't think Page Likes were important? Think again.)

- **Retargeting Traffic to Your Website** (Didn't think driving traffic to those blogs on your site was worth anything if they didn't buy? Hmm...)

- **1% Look-A-Like Audiences** (Facebook has the ability to create an audience of 1% of the world that is most similar to whatever audience you give them... If you're not targeting this audience, you're losing money.)

There are some unique variables within 'Look-A-Like' audiences, but I'd recommend creating them on the following:

- Page Likes

- Website Traffic

- Customers

- Email Subscribers

There are about a million other factors (such as demographics, interests, marital status, job, etc....) that you can use as well!

(If you have a local business, you can target based on geographical location.)

Ads

Your Ad consists of:

- **Text** (This is the caption that appears above your…)

- **Image or Video** (Think scroll stopping!)

- **Headline** (Test different ones. Focus on the one big idea you're trying to communicate or the one primary benefit of what's in it for them.)

- **Link** (You can choose any URL you'd like to send your traffic to.)

- **CTA Button** (There are 10-15 options for what your button says… We typically go with Learn More or Download.)

Here's an example for you:

You use a Facebook Ad to get someone to opt in for your 7-page PDF. They then see a Thank You page with a link to download… and you can include a secondary call to action below the download link.

That could be an exclusive discount not available anywhere else because the only people seeing this are going to be people that you attract through these ads. You use this OTO (One Time Offer) behind your lead magnet and this helps you liquidate the ad spend to be profitable (or at least breaking even).

Yes, you can profitably acquire subscribers and customers through advertising.

MoTip: Start with $5-10 per day. Test multiple ads to multiple audiences. Turn off the ones that aren't profitable. Turn up the ones that are. Find your sweet spot and then scale.

There are many different moving parts to formulating effective Facebook Ads and finding your sweet spot, but what's important is that if you create a product, you must launch, you need to create a funnel, and you need to fill your funnel so that your products sell and your inquiries/applications come in all day, every day.

Recap

Back to that loaded question of 'What do you do?'...

Well, this is what we do.

That's a very quick overview of The MoMachine but I hope it gives you clarity on how all this stuff fits together.

- Create The Website.

- Build Your Email List.

- Get Active on Social.

- Create Valuable Content.

- Package Popular Content into Products.

- Launch New Products/Courses!

- Develop a Profitable Funnel.

- Fill The Funnel with Facebook Ads!

(Can you tell that product launches, funnels, and Facebook Ads excite me the most?!)

About 80% of our time is focused on those three 'gears' of The Machine for our clients, but that doesn't mean the first 5 are not important. Without a solid foundation, the launches, funnels, and ads won't perform nearly as well.

Without a Machine like this in place, you may sell some products initially, but then the sales will drop off and you'll wonder why. It's most likely because you don't have these 8 components of The Machine in place in your business.

To quickly recap, here are the 3 Phases of Building Your Online Business...

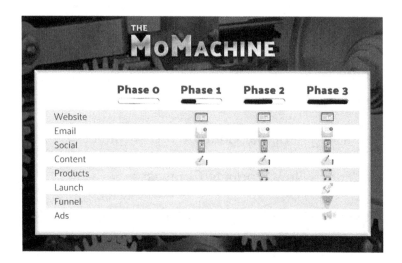

At this point, you should be able to identify which of these 3 Phases you are currently in.

All of the gurus are saying 'Do this. Do that. More of this. None of this.'

From the outside, looking at what they're all teaching is chaotic and it changes all the time.

From the trenches, it's very clear what you need to do (and that doesn't change all the time). That's why I put this book together.

It's simple and it's proven to work, over and over again.

You might not have all 8 pieces of your Machine ready to go today, but I invite you to:

- Do your homework.
- Follow the right people.
- Try new things.
- Trust your intuition.
- Enjoy the process!

That is what we do.

MoTools

This section contains an overview of the Tools that we use on a regular basis to power more than 100+ online businesses!

(For a complete list of the MoTools you can use to build your Machine, visit Matt-Morse.com/Machine/Tools.)

Branding/Design

- Photoshop ($$)
- Canva
- InShot

Website

- Bluehost ($)
- WordPress
- X Pro Theme ($$)
- WooCommerce

Social

- Hootsuite

- Facebook Business Manager
- Facebook Ads Manager

Email Tools

- MailChimp
- ConvertKit
- Mailbutler

Automation

- Zapier
- IFTTT

Collaboration

- Asana
- Slack
- Voxer
- Google Drive
- Google Docs
- Google Sheets

Presentation

- BeLive.tv
- Zoom.us
- EverWebinar

Video

- YouTube
- Vimeo

For a complete list of tools you can use to build your Machine, visit Matt-Morse.com/Machine/Tools! (includes an in-depth, detailed breakdown of each)

Work with Matt

If you **have a team in place** and you want to get 1% better, go to Matt-Morse.com and you will see a few different ways that we can start working together..

If you **don't have a team in place**, want to keep focusing on what you do best, and want everything we just talked about to be done for you, visit Kaifect.com. Fill out the application and we will follow up with you ASAP to discuss how we can take your business to the next level.

It's time to put your brand or business on the map so that you can **maximize your impact** and **leave a legacy** that is much bigger than you and helps a lot of people in a positive way.

Matt Morse

Matt Morse is an innovative entrepreneur, business & marketing coach, agent, #1 best-selling author, and speaker who equips top businesses, authors, speakers, and coaches with the tools and strategies needed to maximize their impact.

There are 6 ways you can work with Matt:

1. The Entrepreneur Lab

A community of innovators and action takers who want to learn, create, and grow together. (If you're in Phase 0, the Entrepreneur Lab is a great place for you to start.)

2. Build-a-Brand Workshop

In-depth live online training course on how to develop and monetize your brand. These 8 weeks will change the landscape of your business and give you a much clearer understanding of the opportunities that you have.

3. Mastermind

An exclusive group of elite entrepreneurs on a mission to

maximize their business and lifestyle. (If you're in Phase 2 or 3, the Mastermind is a great way for you to connect with other like-minded entrepreneurs and stay on the cutting edge.)

4. Speaking

Exciting and inspiring keynote experiences for your organization. If you want Matt to come speak to your team or organization, visit Matt-Morse.com/Speaking.

5. One Day Blitz

An intensive fast-paced day of business development and strategy with Matt. If you want Matt to look at your business in depth and analyze each component of the Machine in your business, the 1-Day Blitz will be the best 24 hours you've had in a long time.

6. Private Coaching

The most exclusive access to Matt. If you want to work with Matt on an on-going basis and have him on speed dial, this private coaching opportunity is guaranteed to improve your business and your lifestyle.

FREE: Lifestyle + Business Self-Evaluator

Identify how Matt can help you to get to the next level by completing this Lifestyle + Business Self Evaluator.

FREE: The MoReport

Want to hear what Matt is working on, what's working and what's not? Get the MoReport delivered to your mailbox every month. This short, handwritten note from Matt is FREE. You just cover shipping & handling to get this report delivered to your mailbox every month. Visit Matt-Morse.com/Report to join The MoReport today!

Kaifect

After investing a lot of time into figuring out what it is that this agency represents, we discovered that, at its very core, it all comes back to continuously improving performance, getting 1% better every day.

The name **Kaifect** stems from the Latin words **kaizen** and **effectus**.

Kaizen means to continuously improve, and effectus is performance. Collectively, we are working relentlessly to get 1% better every day and to help our clients do the same.

Kaifect is a full service marketing agency that helps authors, speakers, coaches, athletes, artists, entrepreneurs, and businesses to maximize their impact. We do it through 9 core pillars:

1. Online Strategy

From concept to execution, we construct and maintain your online plan of attack while providing detailed, actionable reporting to keep you moving forward.

2. Branding and Design

Look great, feel great, perform great. We build recognizable brands, ensure you maintain quality and keep you on the cutting edge.

3. Web Development

We construct websites that are just as clean on the back end as they are on the front. Most importantly, your website will serve a purpose and feed your mission.

4. Social Media

If you're not utilizing social media to connect with and serve your people, it's about time. We specialize in managing platforms, accounts, and creating fresh content that aligns with your brand.

5. Email Marketing

Your most valuable asset as a business is your list. We write clean, engaging copy that speaks directly to your avatar and is an extension of your voice.

6. Content

We remove the obstacles and enable you to create quality, consistent content that is curated and shared to all platforms through our streamlined processes.

7. Products

We turn your knowledge and expertise into valuable products and then capture the attention of your audience through explosive product launches.

8. Marketing Funnels

Scale your time and energy with an efficient and effective sequence that gives your customers what they want when they need it, and start making money while you sleep.

9. Digital Advertising

Now, it's time to fill your funnel. When we work together, your avatar becomes our avatar, and we know how to reach them online.

If you're ready to take your business to the next level, let us help you focus on what you do best...

We'll handle the rest.

With a new client, we start with one specific project that could include any of the components of the Machine laid out for you in this book... The most common projects we start with are:

- building a new website,

- designing/publishing a book,

- launching a new product,

- installing and optimizing your funnel, or

- creating and managing a Facebook Ad campaign.

After successfully completing a project, there are various ways in which we can continue to work together where we handle all of the above for you and manage your Machine while reporting on a monthly basis exactly how it's performing, what's working, and what we can do to improve.

Visit **Kaifect.com** and submit the application to learn more and see if this is a good fit for you and your business.

Gratitude

This is where it begins and ends…

I'm beyond grateful for the opportunities, the coaches, the mentors, the challenges, the wins, and the losses that I've had the opportunity to experience… None of which would be possible without the love and support from so many people over the years.

I'd like to start by thanking **my parents** for always making a tremendous effort to allow me to be around great people, great coaches, and have the opportunities to pursue my dreams and my passions.

My wife Rachel's never ending support of my mission often includes long days and nights working relentlessly to find solutions to help our awesome clients. She has been an incredible support and has contributed in enormous ways.

I'm thankful for **my sister Beth, my brother-in-law Dusty, and their three kids (Braden, Ashlyn, and Tanner)** for their support of everything we pursue. It means the world to me.

I'm thankful for the coaches that I have had the opportunity to be around: **Don Beebe, Brian Shoop, Perry Roth, Ron Polk, and Josh Hopper** to name a few... My coaches at UAB gave me the opportunity to play college baseball, but it was an even greater opportunity to be around them for 5 years, to surround myself with great teammates who would become groomsmen in my wedding and partners in business.

I'm thankful for **Tyler Mims**, a former teammate and groomsmen of mine, who is now my business partner and keeps this Machine rolling.

I'm thankful for our other team members who contribute in enormous ways and play a very critical role in the continual development of the Kaifect agency.

I'm thankful for **our amazing clients** that we get to work with on a daily basis. We work relentlessly to create positive life changing results for them and greatly appreciate their commitment, their loyalty, and their trust in building their business and having their life's work entrusted to us.

I'm thankful for the great leaders and experts in the online marketing and personal development spaces who have had a tremendous impact on my life, my business, my perspective, and continue to inspire me every day: Tony Robbins, Jeff Walker, Tim Ferriss, Brendon Burchard, and Russell Brunson are a few of my favorites. Much of what I have shared with you in this book was inspired by their work and I am forever grateful for the ability to learn from them.

I'm thankful to be alive in times with such great technology and opportunity to connect with other people around the world.

I thoroughly enjoy and appreciate the opportunities to meet new prospects, to learn about their story and to learn about the experiences that they have to share. I've learned something from each individual I've had the privilege to connect with.

I'm thankful for the health and energy I have to be able to do what I do every day.

I'm thankful for the opportunity to work when I want, where I want, with who I want, and I take that very seriously. I do not take it for granted as that freedom is what allows us to continue to improve, innovate, and help more people in bigger and better ways.

People often ask what drives me and how I can keep moving so fast, working so hard....

Gratitude.

That's it.

When I think of the opportunities in front of us and the amount of time and energy that my family, coaches and mentors have invested into my development, I am overwhelmed with gratitude.

That is why I continue to charge on and work relentlessly to continue helping others to the best of my abilities.

Thank You! If you've made it this far, I'm thankful for your interest and desire to keep getting better. Statistics show that **less than 5% of people who purchase a book ever finish reading it**. I'm thankful that you are in that 'less than 5%'!

You were created with a purpose.

There are people waiting to be helped.

It's time for you to step up and impact the world in the way that you know you can.

Simplify the process.

Eliminate the noise.

Focus on the things that matter.

Get The Machine in place so you and your business can serve others at the highest level.

Make that your mission.

Featured Q&A

After explaining all of this to clients and prospects, they usually have one big question they need answered for it to all fit together...

> **Q:** "Is it better to create an individual funnel for each target market if you have a product that can be used by multiple different target demographics?"
>
> -Donald F.
> Denver, Colorado

A: That's a great question. If you don't have a funnel in place yet, I would create one and run multiple targets into that funnel to begin. Once you've got that in place and that's rolling pretty good for you, I would say you can create individual funnels for each target market, because the messaging can be tweaked accordingly. For example, if you're running a funnel to volleyball players, coaches, and parents, you can target them accordingly and have players go to one, coaches go to one, and parents go to another. The messaging on those pages would be very different.

If you're trying to increase volleyball performance, if

you're targeting an athlete, they specifically want to improve their performance. They want to jump higher. They want to become a more consistent player. Your messaging would speak to that.

If it's the same product, but you're marketing to a coach, you would take the angle of saying that this will help your team to do _____.

Then if you're going to the parent, there's different pain points and different benefits to each market. The parent probably wants their athlete to play better so that they're happier, so that they get more playing time, or even earn a college scholarship.

The messaging on each of those should be different.

The back end of the funnel could look pretty similar but I would say that the messaging on the landing page and/or the sales page should be different based on the target. If you don't have a funnel in place, start with one. Optimize it. Get it going. Then, start to test splitting off multiple funnels to multiple audiences.

> **Q:** "What makes a good free opt-in?"
>
> -Lindsey L.
> Fort Lauderdale, Florida

A: There are a ton of good ways to build your list. Typically that's done through a lead magnet, which is something of value that you almost feel like you can charge money for. You're going to give that to them in exchange for their email address, because you are focused on building your list that you might offer a product or service to down the road.

The most popular (maybe the easiest with the least resistance to create) are PDF reports. Maybe a 2-10 page PDF report that is your core teaching, that you know will help create a quick win for them.

That information can be distributed in any number of ways. It could be a 3-video series. We've seen those do really well. It could be a 20-minute audio recording that they need to listen to before every game. It could be a chapter of a book. If you want to make an offer to a book right after that, giving them the first chapter or an excerpt from the book is a good free opt in.

> **Q:** "What kind of follow up sequence do you use after the initial opt in?"
>
> -Mary L.
> New York City, New York

A: This comes back to what phase you're in. If you're in Phase 1 and you're just starting to build your audience and you just have a lead magnet but no products or services yet, I would suggest a brief 3-4 day email sequence. Email them once a day giving value.

Day 1: Give Them The Download

Day 2: Recap + Here's Another Blog You Might Like

Day 3: Most Popular Podcast

Day 4: Follow Us on Social For More

If you're in Phase 2 or 3 and you have some depth to what you're offering, that initial follow up sequence could be up to 7-10 days. You could have an offer built in there. If you have an Evergreen Launch, you could give value for the first 4 days and then do an Evergreen Launch type of sequence from days 5-8. What that means is they are going to get your content for 4 days. You're going to build up great rapport with them, and then you're going to make some sort of a limited time offer for them to take the next step to getting into your business. That might be a book, a video course, or possibly a high end coaching program, but ultimately that initial opt in sequence can be everywhere from one single email that says 'Here's your PDF' to an in-depth 10-day sequence that leads them through everything that you have to offer.

> **Q:** "If I could attend any one live event for personal or professional development, what would you recommend?"
>
> -Marissa L.
> Huntsville, Alabama

A: Tony Robbins' Unleash The Power Within.

…and there's not a close second!

It should be a pre-requisite for any entrepreneur, athlete, or high performer.

> **Q:** "What is the best way to use audio to create content?"
>
> -Don H.
> Montgomery, Alabama

A: Podcasts can be a great way to reach people. If you

don't have a podcast, I would start by focusing on creating video clips or audio clips that you can give in exchange for an opt in or however you bring them in for free.

Get on other people's podcasts! Become a guest on other podcasts in your industry, in your niche that you know have a similar audience to the audience that you are trying to attract. You can them feature those on your site, social accounts, etc...

> **Q:** "I'm looking to begin an affiliate marketing plan for an online course we have coming up. I've never constructed one by myself. Do you have any ideas that you'd be willing to share?"
>
> -Bill N.
> Atlanta, Georgia

A: Affiliate programs are very dynamic, flexible, and unique to the specific situation, but if your website is built with WordPress, there are several WordPress plugins that can do this.

AffiliateWP is the one that I use and it's relatively easy to set up. Then what you're going to do is set the commission percentage that they get if they generate a sale through their affiliate link and you can also provide them with copy that they can paste to their emails to send out to their list, or they could even copy and tweak it, and then send it out to their list.

You want to provide them with the necessary assets, the copy, the graphics, the links, the correct links to promote your products…. essentially making it as easy as possible for them to be an affiliate for your product.

NOTE: I have found that it is more effective to work with 3-10 great affiliates who are bought in, rather than trying to attract 20-40 affiliates that you don't know are really interested in promoting your product or service.

Q: "Should I be using Facebook live broadcasts to drive traffic to my website?"

-Beth B.
Springfield, Illinois

A: Yes. Any way that you can capture attention once you have created value, I believe you should at least experiment with. If you know that your audience lives on Facebook and they love to watch videos, I would highly recommend that you use Facebook live broadcast to do so. There are many benefits to this. The one that I like the most is that you have the ability to download the recording after you've done the live broadcast and you can use that video in other ways. You can embed it on a blog on your website. You could transcribe it into text. Video allows you to be very dynamic in your marketing and builds trust at the same time.

A tool called BeLive.tv allows you to do split screen interviews or even talk show mode interviews (with 3-4 guests) on a single live broadcast. This is great for doing Q&A style interviews, interviewing an expert about your topic, or even getting on other people's Facebook live broadcast. If their page has a significant following and they want to promote your product or service, it would make sense for them to feature you in a Facebook live interview where they talk about their experience with you and their background with you, and open the line up for you to be able to talk about your product and service.

NOTE: If you're going to do Facebook live broadcasts, I would highly recommend the first half of the interview being value based, giving, telling story before you pivot to any type of offer, or product, or service.

> **Q:** "What if I don't have a product to sell?"
>
> -Mikal R.
> Sydney, Australia

A: This is a great question. If you don't have a product to sell or maybe you don't have a website yet, this is a great place to be because I've been through this process so many times now that you're going to really shorten your learning curve and be able to not only create products better and faster but be sure that you're creating the right products. There is nothing worse than not really knowing if you even have a market for that or not knowing if there's anyone who is going to buy that. So the Machine, if nothing else, is going to make sure that you create the right product for the right people at the right time for the right price.

Check Part 5 of the Machine for more information on this. If you'd like help creating your first product, visit MattMorse.com/Machine/Next and submit the application. We'll follow up with you on how we can help you make that happen.

> **Q:** "What software should I use for social media?"
>
> -Ronald P.
> Bute, Montana

A: There are a ton of software tools/apps out there. About 50% - depending on who you are and what you do, it can vary a bit - of your social posting can be automated and the other 50% is going to be live at events, at different speaking engagements, etc… You're also going to be sharing what other people are posting about you.

Again, this comes back to not having to be self promotional, but when you put this Machine in play, you create foot soldiers that are mentioning your work, talking about your products, talking about your events, and that is where you can share those. This also allows you to feature screenshots of people talking about you on social on your sales pages as social proof.

For automated social media scheduling, we typically use HootSuite.

> **Q:** "What is the biggest obstacle you've faced and how did you overcome it?"
>
> -Tamara W.
> Los Angeles, CA

A: The biggest obstacle I've faced is doing everything myself. I've started to overcome that by building a team of people who understand the mission of what we're trying to do and then coach them through the process so I can delegate and focus my time and energy where it needs to be to make the biggest impact.

> **Q:** "What portion of your budget to go to online advertising? (Facebook, Twitter, Instagram, etc...)"
>
> -Rich D.
> Trenton, NJ

A: The goal is to get at least $2 back for every $1 you put in. I'd start with $5-10/day across a variety of different audiences. You'll quickly see which ads and audiences are most effective. Feed the ones that are profitable. Pull out of the ones that aren't. Once you're getting $2+ for every $1 spent, I'd recommend spending as much as possible.

> **Q:** "What first steps did you take on your Mental Game VIP and Leadership VIP projects?"
>
> -Chris C.
> Chicago, IL

A: The first steps in creating the Mental Game VIP + Leadership VIP products were to:

1) Pick topic.

2) Gather a list of questions to ask and 'buzz words'/hot topics to discuss on the interviews. (I did this by talking with others in the industry to know what they would like to learn more about.)

3) Identify and contact possible interviewees.

After the interviews, I had audio recordings transcribed to text, then sorted the text by topic and went through the self-publishing process, gathering support of interviewees to help promote the product once it was available.

Bonus #1: How To Write a Book in 1 Day

Without Writing a Single Word

Ok, there's a little more to it than that… but this process will jumpstart you to getting your next book published:

- **Step #1:** Framework/Outline Your Message

- **Step #2:** Create PowerPoint Slides

- **Step #3:** Narrate The Book While Navigating Slides

- **Step #4:** Send Audio to Rev.com To Be Transcribed

- **Step #5:** Send Transcription to Editor

- **Step #6:** Review & Format Interior

- **Step #7:** Add Photos or Graphics

- **Step #8:** Upload to KDP/CreateSpace

Bonus #2: 2 Steps to Get More Speaking Engagements

You might be reading this, thinking, **"All I really want is more speaking engagements."**

One of the best ways to get more speaking engagements is to create content and put your message out there.

Share your message on **social**.

Share your message through your **blog**.

Share your message through **video**.

Write a book. (A book has been the most effective way that we have found to get more speaking engagements.)

There's 2 ways that we secure more speaking engagements:

#1) Streamlining, organizing, and optimizing the application or inquiry process that you already have so that nothing falls through the cracks. The content that you create with the funnel and The Machine in place is going to naturally lead them there, if that's where they need to be.

#2) Being proactive in reaching out to prospects, letting them know who you are, what you do, and why you'd be a great fit to be in front of their audience. One of the best ways to do that when you reach out to really get their attention is to send them a physical paperback book and say, "Hey, this is me. This is my message. This is what I'm about. If you read this book and you like it, I would love to come share this message with your team or your organization."

If you're interested in having us represent you as a speaker, fill out the form at Kaifect.com and we'll follow up with you ASAP.

Bonus #3: How To Determine Free vs. Paid

So, you're ready to create a new piece of content…

But there's one problem!

You're not sure if it should be free 'blog' content or packaged into a paid book/eBook…

Should it be 1 long free YouTube video… or split up and packaged into a paid video product?

Here's the question I ask clients to help decide if it should be paid or free:

Is this something that you <u>think</u> should be a product, or is this something that you <u>know</u> should be a product?

One word difference. Pretty big distinction.

If you think it should be a product (or aren't sure), then publish it as free blog/social content.

If you know that it should be a product, then it might

be…

Once you've done your homework and know this is a product, then it's time to do some further market research and confirm demand, audience, price structure, etc… and decide if it's feasible.

5 Quick Questions To Help Determine Pricing

- What type of value does your product deliver?
- What are your costs involved?
- What level of demand for your product exists?
- What cost savings will your customer experience as a result of consuming your product?
- What is fair?

If you want me to help you in the content/product creation process, get in the Entrepreneur Lab and let's break it down!

Chances are pretty good that you've got a product inside of you that, with some deep work and split-testing, we can help you position, package, and promote.

Bonus #4: What To Do If You Get Frustrated

So, you're trying to write a new book...

But can't stop thinking about your Facebook Ads....

And wondering if your funnel is still working...

Meanwhile, your inbox is inundated with customer service requests...

And you're still not sure how to track conversion rates on your new lead magnet.

And what about selling on Amazon vs. Shopify vs. Woo?

(Oh yeah, what about split-testing all of your ads?)

Then trying to decide which online course to buy next.

Only to discover that you're not even really sure who your avatar is yet.

...and when the book's done, now what?

Maybe switch e-mail providers and try a new social

automation tool?

If this sounds familiar, I invite you to try this moving forward:

Simplify.

Get one website.

Have one e-mail list.

Use one social media account.

Create one new piece of content each month.

Have one lead magnet.

Write one book.

Run one Facebook ad.

Record one webinar.

Ok, you get the point…

Simplify.

Less is more.

Find what works.

Do more of that.

(or let us do it all for you!)

Bonus #5: 5 Bullets for Your Brand or Business

Use this ammo wisely.

#1) Organize Systems & Processes

If you want to scale a successful agency, you <u>must</u> have your systems and processes written out in detail. Our monthly 'kickoffs' and weekly 'huddles' have helped us to gain great traction and ensure everyone is on the same page.

To **'kickoff'** the first of each month, we pull up a Google Doc and discuss the following questions while taking notes on important insights:

- What went well last month?

- What can we do differently moving forward?

- What needs to be accomplished this month? By when?

- Who is doing what by when?

We go through this process for our agency, and we also

do it for each client as well. (We then pass on our notes to each client along with their monthly analytics report.)

Every Monday, we have a brief **15-minute huddle** to discuss our most important tasks for the week.

NEW: One thing we've begun doing more recently is starting every morning with a **3-minute whiteboard session** where a team member (different each day) writes a question on the board and then we have 3-minutes to fill up as many sticky notes as possible with answers to that question. (This has created some pretty awesome product ideas, business models, creative proposals, etc... as well as helped us overcome challenges!) By the end of the week, the whiteboard is full of great ideas!

You can download our templates for monthly kickoffs, weekly huddles, and daily whiteboard sessions by visiting Matt-Morse.com/Machine/Tools.

#2) Identify Client Wants/Needs

Understanding this is crucial to success as an agency. Each client is unique in their desires, wants, and needs. The decisions you make and projects you pursue with them should be dictated by and line up with the client's desired outcomes.

Start by asking them: **What would make you look back on our work together and say 'Wow - That was incredible!'?**

Reverse engineering (a cool way to say thinking backwards) is an important skill to develop if you are running an agency. Find what it is that you (or the client) want to accomplish. Pick the date it needs to be done by. Then, work backwards to put together a tangible action plan.

PRE-MORTEM: Within the idea of reverse engineering, another helpful tool to add is the 'pre-mortem'... What could cause this to fail? What potential obstacles could arise along the way? Thinking this through in advance (and taking action accordingly) will change the game for you. Also, sometimes a thorough pre-mortem process will result in you discovering that maybe your idea/project is just not feasible. (Well, you just saved yourself time and energy that can now be re-directed elsewhere.)

#3) Explicit Communication

No, I don't mean using foul language. Speak in very clear, easy to understand terms. Let your 'yes' mean yes and your 'no' mean no. Most importantly, do what you say you're going to do. Build up a high level of accountability with yourself.

EXAMPLE: If a client presents a great idea to you, such as… "Hey Matt! I was just thinking about the blog post that received 12,000 visits and 400 comments within the first 24 hours. I really think that I have more content I can add around that post and it seems to be pretty popular. Maybe I can record a video and create a worksheet to go with it?"

An average agency responds with: "Yeah, that's a great idea."

Explicit Communication would be: "I was just thinking the same thing! How about you write up a framework for what that video would consist of and e-mail that to me by next Wednesday? I'll review and send feedback to you by Friday. Then, if you're able to record by the following Friday, I'll have our content creator put together a corresponding worksheet and we can have it all ready to go within 2 weeks. Let me know your thoughts on that. All we'd need from you is a link to the video emailed over by next Friday. If you want to move forward on it, we'll get the wheels in motion on our end."

Does that make sense?

Keep the conversation moving forward.

Using explicit communication will help you to respect the client's time and energy, get more done in less time, create a better finished product, and help all parties involved better understand the situation.

ONE MORE THING: When someone asks you a question, **answer it**.

#4) Monthly Tracking

Provide detailed analytics of what you're doing, the impact it's having, along with actionable summaries of what is working, what isn't, what was accomplished within the past month and what you're focused on in the upcoming month.

Visit Matt-Morse.com/Machine/Tools to see an example tracking template and corresponding summary we provide to each client on a monthly basis.

#5) Overdeliver

Always do more than expected.

Bonus #6: The 2 Most Powerful Tools for MoProductivity

I often get asked about my efficiency and productivity... There are many habits I've developed over the years, but none more powerful than these two:

#1) Inbox0

Living in your e-mail is a great way to get nothing done.

I process my inbox 2x/day.

I have a folder for each client, but then I have the Big 3:

- To Do > 2 Min
- Awaiting Action
- Next Week

So as I go through my e-mails, I use the 4D's to decide what to do with each e-mail:

- Do
- Date
- Delete
- Delegate

NOTE: Most e-mails are getting deleted within 1 second... but I never close my e-mail with a message in my 'Inbox'. (I also never open it without the intent and energy to process all messages.)

If it's less than 2 minutes, I do it.

If it's more than 2 minutes, I either put it into the To Do > 2 Min folder (which I schedule time each day to go through), or if it's not urgent I put it in the Next Week folder (which I go through 1x/week).

The key here is that **I hunt zero**. That allows me to ensure that nothing falls through the cracks and that every email is followed up on within 24 hours.

MORE: Inbox0 is more than just e-mail. I get my text messages, recent calls, voicemails, and Voxer messages to zero every day as well.

#2) Clear to Neutral

Along the same lines of the above, this may feel a little OCD at times but it's allowed us to attack each and every day with a clear mind and great energy.

We are creatures of habit, so you need to be intentional about creating elite habits!

IMO: Clearing to neutral is essential to do in your physical and digital spaces at least once per week.

The first thing we look at during a 1-Day Blitz is your productivity and the systems/processes you use on a daily basis. It's almost always the most productive and valuable part of the day.

To learn more about how you can schedule your 1-Day Blitz, visit Matt-Morse.com/Blitz.

Bonus #7: How This Book Was Written

1. Narrated by Matt Morse.

2. Transcribed by Rev.com.

3. Edited and formatted by Kaifect.

4. Graphics designed by Kaifect.

5. Icons designed by Freepik from Flaticon.

6. Final content reviewed by Kaifect

7. Uploaded to Vellum eBook Creator.

8. Exported and delivered by Kaifect.

9. Converted to print format per KDP standards.

10. Uploaded to KDP.

11. Printed by KDP and Shipped to the Kaifect Fulfillment Headquarters.

12. Packaged and shipped to you from the Kaifect Fulfillment Headquarters.

Made in the USA
Columbia, SC
17 January 2019